THIS BOOK BELONGS TO

Love

Love

www.ingramcontent.com/pod-product-compliance
Lightning Source LLC
Chambersburg PA
CBHW081724220526
45468CB00008B/1971
9781984116819